LAST CALL

STORIES OF A BARROOM
CASTLES SONS' WINDING
ROAD TO REDEMPTION

AL SWAIN

Fulton Books, Inc.
Meadville, PA

Published by Fulton Books 2022

The characters and incidents in this book, although inspired
by actual events, have been fictionalized for dramatic purposes,
and are not intended to depict actual individuals or events.

ISBN 978-1-63985-026-6 (paperback)
ISBN 978-1-63985-027-3 (digital)

Printed in the United States of America

For
Por Meu Amor
Written with Deliberate Intent.

Contents

1. "Here Comes Your Nineteenth Nervous Breakdown" 7

2. We Can Be Heroes 9

3. Why Did You Go to the Police? Why Didn't You
   Come to Me First? 10

4. Snowblowers..12

5. For the Good Times 21

6. In Vino Veritas 22

7. I Started a Bad Joke 25

8. Don't Let Me Down 27

9. Eyes of Green..30

10. Crossroads 31

11. Guns 33

12. Kickin' Bass 34

13. Marine 13...38

14. Jackknife in Your Sweaty Hands 40

15. FTD Lover Boy 43

16. And His Mama Cries...46

17. Puffing on the Mary Jane..48

18. Words Are All I've Got 49

19. In for a Penny...50

20. Hoopah Drives the Boat..51

21. BFF 53

22. She Ain't No "Maid of Honor" 55

23. Upon Us All a Little Rain Must Fall 57

24. I Got a Speech for That 58

25. Melancholy Rock 60

26. Dog Day Sunny Afternoon 61

27. The King(s) of Cool 63

28. Little Darling 64

29. She Thinks I'm Cute 66

30. Music Icons 68

31. Going to Massachusetts 69

32. Gone Girl 72

33. Va Com Deus 73

34. Just Throwing Out the Garbage 74

35. "Sac" 76

36. Bar Fight 78

37. WTF 79

38. What the Cluck 81

39. Take a Look at Yourself and You'll See Others Differently 83

40. G-Man and the Loser Birds 84

41. Take Me Home 85

42. Let It Be 87

43. Get Back to Where You Once Belonged 88

44. The Work Doesn't Stop till the Casket Drops 89

Author's Note 90

"Here Comes Your Nineteenth Nervous Breakdown"

—Rolling Stones

I saw her. I thought we parted ways years ago. And of all places, she was hiding in my spare bedroom, where clutter goes to die. I caught a glimpse of her by an unpacked suitcase from a cruise twenty years ago.

I broke up with this bitch. Yes, me. She was not a real person 'less I seem like a heartless prick. She was the bare bones of a book I was writing over eight years ago. Memoirs, anecdotes, poems, and everything in between.

I didn't want to touch it. Anxiety speared my soul and my spirit. I started to read it. Some of it was good. Most of it was pure dog shit. Writers are creatures of habit. I suspect most of us back this shit up. We'll write it. Maybe it's okay. We'll puff on some marijuana. Now it's pretentious bullshit.

Thousands of pages found a home in my local landfill. Good riddance. Then I'll have a drink or something, and I'm digging through my garbage. Pathetic people, some of us are. For years, I knew that the bones of my book were close by.

I guess because I was always inebriated. I was disillusioned and thought that my book would magically write itself and become a best seller. First of all, I'm not going to blame anyone or anything for my fall from grace. I can't even watch that stupid "intervention" because every motherfucker blames some injury or loss of a loved one on all their woes. Oh, poor me. Fuck you. Pain? I think the only other human alive with more broken bones than me was Evil Knievel. But I was already given to abusing before I got my first splinter.

Loss. Yeah, maybe. My parents died in quick succession. I carry the guilt of not telling them I "loved them" often enough, but I was already drinking heavily while they were still alive.

Honestly, I think it was that I felt like a failure. I never went to college. I was okay to just do my thing, which was not always the right thing. Picking up this book did something to my soul. I felt whole.

I quit everything cold turkey. I'm cut from a different cloth, so I wouldn't recommend this approach to anybody. But it can be done. But it was far from easy. Months without sleeping, eating, and constantly running to the bathroom. All those sleepless nights, all I did was write through trembling hands. Hundreds of pages.

I was afraid to stay in bed with my dark thoughts. I wasn't going to lose my soul. I refuse to spiral like a snake eating its own tail. Doctor, heal thyself. My writings will be my redemption and my salvation.

It's my last call.

4/28/21

We Can Be Heroes

"Pleasant words are a honeycomb.
Sweet to the soul and health to the bones" (Proverbs 16:24).

"But, Lord, you are my shield, my wonderful God who gives me courage" (Psalm 3:3).

Why Did You Go to the Police?
Why Didn't You Come to Me First?

My ol' man brought me to the bar every day when I was a kid. I'd sweep the floors, and luckily, I'd find some change. And it went straight into the pinball machine. I had a high score on every machine that rotated through there. I also suspect Pops threw change on the floor the night before as an incentive to sweep. Anyways, it worked.

So growing up there, in the seventies, was a real learning experience. You learn about life, death, and the streets.

Real hardened men. Battle tested. Veterans. People that could clear bars. Just for the fun of it.

World War II guys like Dagget and Herbie. Dagget was already getting on in age, and the booze finally got the best of him. But he would always talk about how he and his friends absolutely hated the Japanese after Pearl Harbor.

Herbie, nobody told this guy anything, especially to leave the brawling to the younger guys. Even in his sixties and seventies, he was a force to be reckoned with. I can still see him telling guys half his age, "Which way do you want to fall?" Priceless.

Tuffy? Well, let's just say he earned his nickname. Like Vin Diesel in the movie, *Knockaround Guys, 500*.

Lastly, Domingos. A cautionary tale of someone who became a self-made millionaire. And lost it all to alcohol, drugs, divorce, and shady friends.

I remember the first time I've seen a gun. Domingos pulled out a shiny pocket pistol. Opened the front door and "BOOM!" Fucking the coolest thing this ten-year-old had ever seen.

That bullet must have gone straight over the factory, across the river, and landed in the Century House parking lot in the next town over.

These people. They handled their business. They were loved. And they were feared.

Now they're all gone.

RIP:

- P. D.
- H. P.
- C. M.
- D. B.

4/27/21

Snowblowers

(A love-hate story)

Snowblowers. Yes, the contraption that throws that fluffy white stuff that clogs up our driveways and sidewalks.

Where do I start? How's about from the fucking beginning.

Many winters ago, my ex-brother-in-law called offering to sell me a brand-new snowblower for $200. I told him I'd look at it. If it's everything that he said it was, maybe I'd give him a $100. Maybe. Figuring he was short on rent, needed to make a charitable donation to the church, or just wanted to get high. It meant nothing to me, and I could have cared less.

So he shows up with this snowblower, and she's a just fall-off-the-truck cream puff. I'm talking all the bells and whistles, six speed forward, three reverse, electric start, and even a fucking headlight.

Where it came from? Don't care, and I certainly didn't want to know. I'm thinking he needed that money for the church because I pulled out that crisp $100 bill, and with a quick handshake, he ran off into the night. Probably in a hurry to do good deeds with his newfound wealth.

So now I am the proud owner of a brand-new snowblower. Did I mention it had a headlight and electric start? Believe that shit? Electric start? No more cord pulling for this guy. What a winter! Not one fucking snowflake, and I was dying to take that baby for a spin. But I live in New England, so be careful what you wish for.

So I wake up one morning the following winter, and there it was in all its glory. Like the bastard white whale of Moby Dick, "Thar she snows!" And snows, and snows, and snows.

Two feet of the white stuff and, boy, was I ready. As fucking ready as I've ever been. I pushed that start button, and in no time, I was throwing snow twenty to thirty feet into the crisp winter sky. When I was done with my double-wide driveway, I went and did my neighbor's double-wide driveway. Then the old lady's driveway next door. Don't forget my wheelchair-bound friend who lives with his elderly mother. Pretty soon, I did half the block on the arm. I think one ol' lady gave me a bag of oatmeal cookies. Not sure, but I'm sure of this much, it wasn't fucking weed.

It wasn't long before my shiny new toy turned into a curse. Doing the whole block for cookie crumbs loses its appeal fucking quick, and I was looking for an out. Could I tell people my snowblower ran away? Had some terminal disease and needed bed rest? I needed an excuse. Something, anything, so that I wouldn't have to blow that goddamn snow any fucking more. Fucking ex-brothers-in-law.

But alas, help did come, and it was perfect. My ailing father has had the same pull cord snowblower from the 1970s. Yeah, from the last fucking Ice Age, and this thing was a beast.

When he heard mine had an electric start, he couldn't believe it. "Believe," I said! "I'll even bring it by your house tomorrow personally. It's yours, Pa. Free!" My dad likes free anything. Coupled with free delivery. Fucking bonus. "Good riddance, snowblower! Make sure you write now, you hear!"

Now this is still a true story. About a month later, maybe even less, my long-suffering wife's mother and father are moving (downsizing actually). They're moving from a bigger house to a smaller house. Where happenstance would have it that he would have to lighten his belongings.

So the actual wording is neither clear nor paramount in my soggy brain, but it goes something like this, "Hey boy!" (He refers to me as "Hey boy," which is respectfully acceptable to me).

So one more time, "Hey boy, you got a snowblower?"

"Hell no!" I replied.

Apparently, I didn't enunciate the "*hell*" part vehemently enough because before I could utter another word…

"Come on down. You're the new owner of a brand-new second-hand snowblower!"

"Goddamn it!"

For marrying his daughter, I would have been happy with a dowry of two chickens and a goat. But *no*. My gift for stealing away his daughter is another fucking snowblower. These things are falling out from the sky like Moses's plagues, frogs, locusts, pestilence, snowblowers.

If I was truly in need of a snowblower, I would have to trudge down to my local Home Depot, drop a grand, and bada bing! Snowblower in the back of my pickup. But this was something darker, a cruel joke the universe was playing on me, and my hell is a frozen hell of a million snow-covered driveways and sidewalks of old ladies and their fucking oatmeal cookies.

So once again, I'm picking up another hunk of steel. Did I mention I have a bad back? Fractured or totally exploded *C*s and *T*s held together with "Harrington rods," glue, and screws. "Story for another day, peoples!"

Rewind… I'm throwing the snowblower in the back of my truck. Panicking about how I'm going to sneak this fucking snowblower into my garage without a hundred old ladies seeing me. And you better believe old ladies don't miss a thing. They live to look out windows. Then they live to call each other up and say, "Guess who's got another fucking snowblower?"

So I drove home, closed my eyes, and half resigned to my fate and the other half hoping I could just wish it away into the cornfield. I prayed and I prayed, and when I finally opened my eyes, *poof!* A glimmer of hope and hope has a name, and his name is "Snappy Pappy!" A budding landscaper with one rake and a borrowed weed whacker with no string.

So under the cloak of darkness, I make a devil's deal with the Snappy. He gets one free snowblower with the caveat that *every* time it snows, he clears out the front of my driveway, so the wife and I can get our cars out. Very agreeable to him.

Great! I think to myself. "Now take this fucking thing out of my sight now!" I yelled in earnest.

So I'll fast forward a few years, and my negotiated upon agreement with Mr. Snappy Pappy is still holding but cracks are appearing in our acquaintanceship.

Snappy Pappy is a small-time self-made landscaper that got himself in the "*biz*" by poaching a few clients from his previous employer. He has gone from a one rake-and-pony town to a stable off. To the best of my knowledge, an inventory of one lawn mower, one tired rake, the same stringless weed whacker, and yes, my adopted snowblower.

Now for the next few years, we've had some sporadic snowfalls and keeping within our agreement, Mr. Snappy Pappy has always done my driveway first before making a beeline to every old lady's house in the community, where he made a nice fortune for minimum effort. "What? No oatmeal cookies?" Soulless bastard. Taking advantage of hapless old ladies. Fucking wannabe a landscaper making $75 per driveway for thirty minutes of toiling in the snow with my fucking snowblower.

Now the wheels in my head are turning, and I'm going to shake Howard Hughes down faster than Vito Corleone wets his beak.

So I tell Mr. Snappy Pappy that I'm impressed with all the commerce he's making from his new profession. (All thanks to me!) It would be a show of good faith or in his best interest to pay it forward and let me hold one of his envelopes before an avalanche of frosty knuckles befalls his delicate face. This is still a true story if I may reiterate.

So Mr. Snappy Pappy ponders his options for a second and then he runs a hundred miles an hour to my house. No kidding, faster than a jackrabbit being chased by a snow owl. So he runs to my house, and he's crying. Under real, actual tears, he pleads with my long-suffering wife about his dilemma, or what I call a misunderstanding. By the time I trudge through the snow back to my house, Snappy has already run away again. Only warm tears seared into the freshly fallen snow are the only proof of him ever being there. So now "long-suffering wife" is throwing around ugly words like "bully," "racketeer," and "extortionist!"

"Baby, baby, baby! It wasn't anything resembling, sordid, or dis-reputable. I was just doing good deeds."

"Oh yeah?" (With a cynical look.)

"I was only soliciting tax-free donations for the 'Benevolent Neighborhood blah something Society'?" (I quipped in my defense.)

She rolled her eyes with suspect loathing. (You know the look I'm talking about?) But what do I care? I've lived through scarier looks and still came out the other side unsullied.

Fast forward to the 2014–2015 winter. Brutally cold on record snowfall. To the best of my recollection, it snowed a few feet every week. After one particularly bad snowstorm (actually, a blizzard), we were buried under three feet. Snow drifts as high as six-plus feet. No kidding. I had to find a Corolla parked in my driveway by gently prodding with the handle end of a shovel near the spot I last remembered it being parked. It was that deep. Now the Corolla was off the road for the winter, so I could have cared less about unburying it from its frozen hibernation. But I and the wife do have four-by-four Chevys which we do have to free. These vehicles are our lifeblood that we use to get to and from work, shopping, etc…

So "you," the reader, are clearly aware of my disdain and complete detest for snowblowers. As far as I'm concerned, I could care less if my driveway is cleared of snow. We got our four-by-four vehicles and a curbside mailbox. There's absolutely no reason for anybody to be sashaying up my driveway. If I and the missus fall on our butts (and we have), then that's our own fault. But having the trucks make it simple to get in and out. Easy breezy Japanesey. Except when the city plow trucks leave a deep snowy berm at the very entrance of our driveway. I'm not about to shovel four feet of heavy snow. "Hell no!" Not with my back. Nor am I going to chance driving over it and tearing out my exhaust or other expensive undercarriage thingies (i.e., Murphy's law).

So I ask myself, "Where's Mr. Snappy Pappy?" and "Why is the front of my driveway unpassable?" I do a meticulous scan of the frozen horizon that has buried my neighborhood. I know it's there, but it's not so much a house as it is a person. One particular person, and I scan like an eagle looking for my quarry and nope, maybe, *yes!* Mr. Snappy Fucking Pappy!

The other thing I see is a bunch of envelopes stuffed in his back pocket. Probably full of old lady social security gold. Let's not forget that I gave him this snowblower for free to do whatever he wishes as fucking long as he cleans the very front of my driveway first. That's it, simple! Once that simple task is completed, then you have my blessing. By all means, go forth and overcharge grandmas. The sounds of hips breaking on black ice cut through me like fingernails on a chalkboard. (I take the last joke back.) I help the elderly, not take advantage of them.

So I collectively walk over to Mr. Pappy in a very calm and unassuming manner. He was halfway through his second job when I inquired as to why he would see fit to blatantly disregard and default on our orally agreed upon contract. Out of concern, maybe his oversight was due to some brain aneurysm, and perhaps, he wasn't in his full capacities and was in need of medical attention.

"Yo Snappy, what's up?" (I say authoritatively but nonthreatening just the same.)

He replies back through hat and glove, knowingly aware of exactly what I'm talking about. "I'll put you on the list." (With a smirk.)

I'll put you on the list. I'll put you on the list. I'll put you on the list. (Letting my brain absorb what I can't imagine I'm hearing.)

"You're going to put me on the list? YOU ARE GOING TO PUT ME ON THE LIST?" I shout out rabidly.

Snow drifts are avalanching off rooftops. Birds of winter are leaving the cover of trees and taking flight.

"You don't put me on lists! I put *you* on fucking lists!" I shriek wild with exasperation.

I repossessed his snowblower and for the added shame, made him put it in front of my garage door. Head slung low and deflated. I didn't even give him the opportunity to finish whomever driveway he was working on at the moment in time. I heard he had to borrow a plastic shovel from the homeowner just to finish the job, and he hurt his back too. Oh, poor thing! Karma's a bitch, baby!

I sold that snowblower the next fucking day for a paltry $20 to one of Snappy Pappy's adversaries, "Wily Willy." I didn't even want the twenty dollars. I only sold it because I could.

Good Riddance! Good riddance to snowblower number two and to Snappy Pappy with his sore back.

Hello to Patrick O'Googlieye (definitely not his real name). But my Irish pain-in-the-ass good friend. He's my first customer of the day, and we vent and gossip like two old ladies. Ol' Patrick is a true green Irish-me prick. If there are other patrons here, he will always part on this note, "I would say it was a pleasure, but I would be lying!"

"Okey dokey, see you tomorrow."

So Patrick has been throwing around the idea that he should get a snowblower for his house. He's got issues with neck vertebrae among other ailments. Both physical and mental. "Haha!" The pen is mightier than the sword. Now the mere mention of the word "snow-blowers" makes me feel about as warm as taxes and juggling three chainsaws blindfolded.

So this one Sunday morning, some enterprising neighborhood youths came in and said something. (If you guessed they got a snow-blower for sale, give yourself twenty points.) I'll try and write down the actual pre-negotiation back-and-forth banter to the best of my recollection.

"So we got a snowblower for sale!"

(Drip.) That's the sound of my ears starting to bleed.

"I'm all set with snowblowers," I quickly reply with a hint of disgust.

"It's new. Only four hundred bucks."

"Ha, not even for free!" I say.

The lead enterprising youth says, "It's brand new! Three hundred bucks?"

I look over at Patrick, and I can see his interest is piqued, and he wants me to negotiate this thing to an agreeable monetary deal.

So I counteroffer, "I'll look at it and if it's as 'new' as you say, $200 cash money."

The youth smiles and says, "Yes."

So I tell the wife give me two hundred bucks, watch the bar, and I'll be right back.

"I thought you hate snowblowers?" she says, bewildered.

"I do. C'mon, Patrick, we're taking your truck. I know you're the one that really wants to eyeball this thing, so why should we be playing pass the snowblower from truck to truck?"

So off we go following these kids in Patrick's truck. We go to this three-decker tenement, and we are on guard.

"Where's the snowblower?"

"It's up on the third floor," says the kid.

Patrick and I give each other the look. God forbid somebody steal their ill-gotten snowblower. Allegedly.

So Patrick and I trudge up three floors, and all our senses are on high alert. You never know what you're walking into. I felt reasonably safe but still, you can never be too careful. People have been killed for a lot less than two hundred bucks.

Now we walk into this apartment and... *ta-dah*! Another brand-new cream puff. This thing has never even been started up. The little nipples on the tires. Impeccable paint. This thing has never seen weather. I look over at Patrick, and he definitely wants it. He's whispering at me, he'll pay me $200 and a little extra. You better believe. I didn't come up here for my health.

I tell the kids, "Bring her down the three flights of stairs, and I'll take it!"

I do this all the while containing my excitement because this is, without a doubt, a deal or a steal. I say a steal because once again, where it came from, don't care and certainly don't want to know. Plausible deniability.

I and O'Googlieye just made the buy of the year. He was content and I was happy. I made a few bucks and flipped it in under two seconds. Priceless.

"By the way, Patrick," I say. "The wife wants us to stop off at the sandwich shop because she ordered some breakfast bagel something or other."

"Sure, no problem," he said.

We felt good. I made a couple of bucks, and he got a brand-new snowblower for a mere fraction of the cost of buying one at the hardware store. You can't beat them third-floor discounts. Smiles, everyone. Well, our smiles were short-lived.

While backing up to park outside the sandwich shop, the snowblower obscures O'Googlieye's line of sight, and he just barely taps the front bumper of this twenty-plus-year-old Honda with his trailer hitch. No kidding. This car was a piece of shit. The bumper was held in place with wire. All we did was leave a small mark squarely on the front license plate. We never even touched the actual bumper.

"I'm sure it's cool, Patrick."

But it wasn't. The proud owners of this piece of shit insisted on trading insurance information.

Mama always says, "It's best not getting the police involved when you got a snowblower of questionable lineage in the back of your truck." That mama, she's a wise one.

So now, when you figure in the cost of insurance and the yearly surcharge of $100 for five years, that snowblower ended up costing him the same amount as if he had gone to the hardware store instead of a third floor, five finger discount outlet.

Karma is a bitch, and my hate for snowblowers accumulates like the driven snow.

Speech

> I'd like to thank the five pencils that gave their lives
> to write the longest chapter of this book to date.
> (Kar-ma (noun) Another word for bad luck)

For the Good Times

I found this song on YouTube. And I say found. Because I haven't heard it in thirty-five-plus years. This song was on all the fucking time. We had everybody walk through those doors.

From factory workers to factory owners. And they all got nostalgic after a few seven and sevens.

Damn…we even had a half dozen cops come in. Some are still in uniform. Some are in plain clothes. Some are still on the clock.

It was a different time. No cell phones, no cameras, and a handshake was your bond.

There are people I can still remember. Not their names but their faces.

But what's my story? Oh yeah, a song. "For the Good Times." They Ray Price version. Not my man, "Al Green."

So the record drops, and before Ray Price could get out the first verse, "Don't look so sad, I know it's over."

Pops would already have a girl on his arm. Dipping and twirling on our dance floor.

This guy had game. Girls, I've noticed, love a good dancer and he was "Fred Astaire."

My poor mom.

The ol' man cried every day after her passing. Until they were finally buried side by side.

Together forever.

In Vino Veritas

Till death do us part. She will be my forever sweetheart. Sometimes, my wife is feeling down. And out of the blue, she'll ask if I will ever leave her. I usually pause at this junction to play on her self-doubt. Especially if I've had a few Bacardi Cokes, you know? The raised eyebrow, drunken, contemplating face…yeah, that one.

"Hell no! You're stuck with me!" I proclaim reassuringly.

Honestly, I've secretly often wondered if she would be the one to leave my fucked-up ass. Let's keep that one close to the vest, shall we?

But I, Al Swain, believe that I have unlocked the secret to women. Yes, the holy grail to the perplexity of the opposite sex. Many men have only found befuddlement in their quest for the truth.

Under normal circumstances, I would stipulate some kind of nondisclosure…paperwork would be in order. But since you were kind or generous enough to buy my book of true, contemporary musings, I feel compelled to give you my utmost, honest candor on the wily female species.

Okay, you ready? Because this information can be overwhelming to mere mortals.

Bottom line…

Women want a "PROVIDER" and a "PROTECTOR." That's it… simple.

Let's begin with PROVIDER. Ten thousand years ago, provider meant you had a comfortable cave, and you could spear dinner from one hundred feet away.

Second, PROTECTOR…that translates into saving your girl from the caveman down the block. The one trying to woo your woman because maybe he has some cool wall art. Original charcoal Picasso's of caribou. Very nice indeed. Plus, the bear rugs give it a nice, warm, homey feeling. "Fung shui" that fucking abode.

Perhaps he just simply wishes to steal her away the old-fashioned way. Forget cave paintings.

"Utzi dragged my bitch away by the hair last night!" Fucking Utzi. The balls on that Neanderthal.

Utzi aside…being a protector can be as straightforward as spearing, say, a lion. A lion full of hunger pangs. A lion that was stalking and ready to pounce on your beloved, cave-dwelling paramour(s).

There goes date night! And I was going to make popcorn or pop maize.

Bad jokes aside, all this translates seamlessly into modern times.

PROVIDER…nice house, plenty of money, refrigerator stocked, baby's got new shoes, minivan to take the kids to soccer practice. You still with me?

PROTECTOR…unless you're superwealthy, no woman wishes to be saddled with a spineless wimp.

And it's all Darwinian. It's all been proven. Only the strong survive. That held true ten thousand years ago. And it still holds water today.

One last thing…it doesn't hurt to play a little "hard to get." That whole fruit-of-the-forbidden-tree thing. Drives some people crazy when they can't get what they didn't know they needed.

I'm *never* taking off my wedding ring. Don't look at me. Look at me.

To everybody else, don't be the kiss of death. You know what I'm talking about? The creepy/stalker type.

Yeah, you are that ogle and stare. Ogle and stare and talk nonstop. Usually about how your mother wants you out of her cellar.

Take your "*no*" and beat it. Move far away and lament about love lost to whomever you think is listening.

Honestly, I've had two stalkers. It's not fun. These people's brains are wired wrong, and they're just fucked up. And I'm a man, so it must be a nightmare for a woman.

Speech

I feel sorry from the bottom of my heart to anybody who finds themselves alone and longing for companionship at our age. I truly believe that all of the "good ones" are taken. Sometimes, it's better to be "single and happy" than "in a relationship and miserable."

I Started a Bad Joke

So I used to work nights at the bar. After lights out, the real fun began. I'll say, "Lock the front door." Lights went off. Now we can have real fun.

Usually, it'll be me. A few "birds" and a loyal guy friend or two. Let's call it a Monday night.

Okay, there were a lot of stories from those nights. I'm choosing to let some stay between only those involved and will excuse my train of thought for now and tell a story of something done in haste without thinking that it was funny as hell for thirty seconds till cooler heads prevailed.

Now Snappy. Yes, the snowblower guy. He's okay. Loyal as shit. Why did I always mess with this kid? I don't know. In sober reflection, I think I was an asshole full of booze and testosterone.

So what was the joke? Okay, so these snow bunnies and two friends needed cigarettes. Those tooters love to chain-smoke. Ugh! "She tasted like cigarettes, Lieutenant Dan" (Forrest Gump).

So it's no secret that Snappy's close friends know that he can't read or spell very well. Borderline illiterate. Now the "heads" need cigarettes. Three different brands, simple. I still remember two packs of Marlboro, one Marlboro Light, and one Newport.

Snappy saying it over and over because he's our default gopher. He just can't get it right.

I say, "Look, I'll make it nice and easy for you. I'll just write it down on this piece of paper. Just give it to the attendant."

Great. We unlocked the door and let him out into the dark of the night with a note in hand.

I can't remember who remarked about Snappy's poor recall memory.

But at that second, I said, "I think I fucked up."

"Why?"

"That note I gave him, it said, 'This is a robbery!'"

Haha. Then we all got quiet.

"Somebody go stop the kid before he drives away."

"Now!"

We caught him in the nick of time. Didn't tell him what the note said and handed him the correct one under the guise we left a particular brand out.

What a shit show that would have been.

"There shall no evil happen to the just: but the wicked shall be filled with mischief" (Proverbs 12:21).

Don't Let Me Down

Sorry. I've let a lot of people down.

Sorry, Dad, for making you lie for me in a deposition. The ex-wife was angling me for more child support. I would have easily have given it to her if she would have let me see my babies. So he told those fucking lawyers he bought me my Cadillac, Corvette, and a brand-new Harley-Davidson Fat Boy.

He wouldn't ever, in his lifetime, buy his firstborn son a motorcycle. Especially after all the car crashes I was in. Months spent in a Boston hospital learning how to walk again. Half of my body was being held together with rods and metal. Two long rods in my back, which reminds me every morning of my life with crippling pain. RIP Johnny. I fucking told you, "Slow the fuck down."

I'm also sorry, Dad, for my lifestyle. You never asked what I was doing because you didn't want me to lie to you.

But I did enjoy drinking with you every weekend at your bar. Good thing Mom never asked any questions either. You were a great man! My hero! And my hero was flawed too. "I love you, Mom and Dad."

"Sorry, Johnny." I should have never asked you to drive when we were both drinking all day in the sun at that party. "Sorry to your family, Johnny." I never had the courage to say sorry to them. You were their only son. Also, your family disintegrated with your passing.

Sorry to the people I told to "*fuck off*" when they called for a donation. I answered that fucking phone every day, and it was always somebody asking for money. I'm pretty sure half of them were scamsters. I drank a lot. Sorry to the real people. I do donate to St. Jude's Children's Hospital and all animal shelters. I stopped buying

$2000 German shepherds sired by Schutzhund III pure breeds. Now I exclusively adopt shelter dogs. As of this writing, Sunny is looking at me. She knows I'm in pain writing this chapter. Sunny is my pit bull rescue. She is the sweetest dog. She lets my infant granddaughter poke, prod, bite, and do whatever she likes to her. I trust this dog. She's our baby. And she trusts me!

Sorry to Al S. RIP. He came to me in need. His need was $200. So I told him "No problem." Vig is 50 percent. Weekly! Thinking he would fuck off and leave me alone. But he was good with that. I was shocked. Oh well, I'll make an easy extra $100 bucks next Friday.

But when next Friday came, all he had was the one hundred bucks. And he came in *every* Friday with my one hundred bucks. For the next ten months until around Christmas, I was feeling generous and cut him loose. I made close to $4000. And I knew deep down how much I wronged him. My hair-trigger proclivity for violence always kept them towing the line. I went too far with this one. Until the day I finally freed him, he thanked me sincerely every Friday.

Sorry to Jeff A. RIP. I can't remember what he did to me. He was twice my age. I was just a kid, and I smacked him up good. I can still see him on the floor, twisted up and tangled between the bar stools. And if that wasn't enough. I went to his work one day. I popped the hood on his car. I switched all his spark plug wires around. This fucking guy still manages to drive to my bar after work.

"Jeff, you look troubled, something wrong?" I say fully aware of what's troubling him this day.

"My fucking car. Backfiring all the way here," he says.

Poor Jeff. No wife. No kids. His only family was a bad coke habit and drug dealers. I'm sorry. I should have thrown you some help and a friendly ear. Instead, I threw you a flurry of fists.

And a very, very sorry to my wife. All you ever did was love me, and I just kept on hurting you. In my life, I love you more.

After my disastrous first marriage, I vowed to myself I would never let another woman wound me, so I went on a mission to not let another woman emotionally pain me.

I tried hard to make my second wife go away. But you never left. Never called the police. Never wavered. You saved me. In more ways than you know.

Sorry to everybody else that I cared for and hurt. Same certain truths and pain I pressed on people I will carry with me always.

"I am the one who forgives all your sins, for my sake; I will not remember your sins" (Isaiah 43:25).

But there are certain people I will never forgive. Those who bear false witness. And for what? A few dollars. I smiled when I heard you ****. We all toasted your demise. Burn M.F.

On the advice of my attorneys, I got five words for you.

Statute of limitations…and allegedly.

3/16/21

Eyes of Green

Hearts adrift.

Hope you C.

It wasn't meant to be.

Crossroads

Do you ever think about all the random people that intersect our lives? People that we have never met and will never meet again? But because of that chance encounter, a life is irrevocably changed forever.

It was Monday, March 8, 2021. For some reason, I opened up the local newspaper. In my opinion, it's nothing more than a rag. But this liberal rag has some useful purposes. Such as lining the bottom of my birdcage. Poor bird deserves more respect than to shit on this fake news propaganda. But I'm getting sidelined.

I randomly flipped through the newspaper, and there on the obituary page was a name I heard once before. I didn't know this person, but he and I met unknowingly at a critical juncture in time.

His name was Det. Sgt. Franklin A. Eccleston. Another police officer at the scene of the accident told me some years later that this officer above here mentioned, held my hand and my head still because I was supposedly thrashing around.

Good thing too. I had a broken neck and back, along with a dozen other fractures and injuries. All I could remember as I came in and out of conscientiousness was, "Stay still, son. We're going to get you out of here. You're going to be okay." Which couldn't have been farther from the truth.

Let me tell you something. If any of you have lost someone from a terrible wreck or some other unfortunate accident, be comforted because you (I) don't feel a thing.

And here is another interesting nugget. While on the fence between life and death, while my brain was searching desperately for what little oxygenated blood was left in my body, my soul was raised up and I saw myself lying in that ambulance drenched in blood.

Paramedics were doing what they do. I saw us going down the highway. Go through the red light on Route 6. I saw the pond behind Buttonwood Park. Took a left at the green light. Then I don't remember nothing again until I was in the emergency room surrounded by all these doctors and nurses.

Now the pain begins. And a new chapter of my life starts. Now a few days later, I am lying in this hospital bed, immobilized and doped up to the max.

Now that doctors are throwing around words like, "Maybe and hope for the best." I'm not knocking my local hospital, but I believe my injuries were a little above their pay grade. So my father doesn't settle for maybe. He wants to hear someone say, "Yes, your boy will walk again."

The next thing I know, I'm hit with a massive dose of Hydromorphone and put in an ambulance. Off I went to Boston. The minute I got there, I knew that I was in a whole new level of Rolls Royce health care.

This is where I meet my next savior. I'll never forget his name. Dr. Peter F. Sturm. Chief of Orthopedic Surgery. The good doctor microwaved me in MRI machines for two weeks straight. Then he told my father the words that he and my mother prayed for, "Yes, your boy will walk again!"

I saw my father cry for the first time in my life when I took my first step six weeks later.

R.I.P. Det. Sgt. Franklin Eccleston

3/24/21

32

Guns

Guns.

Love them.

I can field strip a Glock model 17 pistol blindfolded in under thirty seconds.

I should also caution to put it back together without the blindfold.

Last thing you want to do is put the recoil spring in backward. What would happen? I don't know. Maybe the gun will blow up in your hand. That's one possibility.

The way this world is going. My new mantra is "Stock up on guns and bullets!"

My friend is one of them preppers. He buys those "ready-to-eat" meals online and stocks up on silver coins.

"What about a gun?" I ask inquisitively.

"Don't have one," he says.

"So what's to stop someone like me from taking your food and silver?" I ask, super curious now.

"You wouldn't do that." He laughs out loud.

"Yes, I would. Just kidding!" No, I'm not!

Speech

I'd like to thank the Second Amendment for giving free men the right to bear arms.

A man is only three days of hunger away from turning into an animal, and when and if it comes to somebody going to hurt mines or steal mines.

Well, I already know what I will do.

Kickin' Bass

R. P. and I have been friends since day one. We were in kindergarten together. We think alike. We like the same things.

One night, we went up to Providence and got into the premier gentleman's club. The Foxy Lady.

We were seventeen and it was a school night. I still got the T-shirt. It's four sizes too small for me now, but it looks good on the wife.

Besides sneaking into strip joints, our true shared passion was fishing. We were diehards. Before we even had cars, my mother would pack up sandwiches, and we'd chase the schools of fish up and down the beaches.

In our twenties, we discovered a sweet fishing hole hidden away behind a berm on the backside of a construction company's parking lot.

We'd fish there every Thursday. We'd have top-of-the-line Penn Reels on ugly sticks and the best line, and we were super secretive of what tackle we would independently use.

"What size hook are you using? You use a wire leader?"

"None of your business."

Priceless, I would think to myself.

We would drink our beer and smoke our weed and just wait for that special moment when a twenty-pound striper would bend our poles right over. This was saltwater, muthafuckers. We didn't fuck with the baby freshwater fish. I'm sure there's a big fish in fresh water. But salt water…there's fifty-, sixty-, even seventy-pound cows out there. We've had our poles bent over so hard sometimes that our poles would fucking break.

One particular night, the fishing was so good that we went through three tide cycles. That's eighteen hours. We were high on the rush and maybe other things too. Either way. We absolutely fucking loved it.

Then one day, the "hole" was closed down. Dredging was going to start, and our beloved secret fishing spot was gone. Just like that.

So what did we do? I bought a boat. A twenty-three-footer. Walk around. We painted and dubbed her "*Kickin' Bass*." She even had a cabin. I had it moored at a marina with free electricity and cable. It doubled as an apartment. But we didn't waste our time at the dock. Every penny we had went into that gas tank. We went out every fucking day. Trolled Clark's Cove for bluefish on weekdays and, on weekends, we'd steam out past the Elizabeth's Island and headed straight for Martha's Vineyard.

Why? Because that's where the big fish are.

So this one day, I took out my lawyer buddy. He wasn't really a lawyer but a legal secretary. He knew many good attorneys and got me out of a few jams. He was pretty useful. Until he wasn't. This guy was moving a bit of product to all his lawyer friends and selectmen. Then I found out he's name-dropping. Telling people that I am his brother and shit. Muthafucka! Never use our names. And that was the end of his usefulness.

But before that day, we used to take him out on the boat. What a pain in the ass. He'd be yelling at passing boats, "Tack, buddy!" R. P. would look at me. This guy thinks this is a sailboat.

"You see that big bulky thing hanging off the stern? That's a motor, you dumb fuck."

Another day, me and R. P. took out "Cappy." That was our nickname for him. A slur for captain, which he was far from. We had some seas. Two, three footers.

So Cappy keeps saying, "We got some rollys. It's really rolling. We got some rollys. Huh, R. P.? It's rolling."

R.P. blows his top. "Say rolly one more fucking time, muthafucka!"

"We got some rollys."

Oh shit! He did it. I know R. P., I saw it in his eyes. He's thinking, *Let's throw this fucker over the side and be done with him.*

Cappy didn't know how close he came to sleeping with the fishes.

Luckily, cooler heads prevailed. Plus, we didn't want to have to buy another anchor and chain. We dropped his ass off at the dock and never looked back and never again answered his calls.

Goodbye, dumb wannabe lawyer. Hello, Snappy. This kid is a walking cliché.

"You got money for gas?" I would ask.

"No."

"Okay. We run out of gas and you're rowing."

"Where's your oars?"

"We don't have any."

Now we're using heavy gear. Titanium eyelets. Wire line. We weren't playing.

Zzzz! Fish on! Snappy asked if he can reel it in. I guess. It's only my boat and my pole. But what the hell. I and R. P. have already caught and released hundreds of fish this season.

"Yeah, go ahead. Knock yourself out."

Now he's reeling in a bluefish. The piranha of the Northeast waters. Pound for pound, one of the strongest fighting fish around and with razor-sharp teeth that have bitten many careless fishermen's fingers clean off.

Now I'm calmly explaining to Snappy that when you bring the fish over the side, lay it on the deck first, less it spits out the hook and it flies up a hundred miles an hour into your hand.

Yep. I'll save some writing. You guessed it. This kid has a huge hook embedded deep into the meaty part of his palm.

Oww! His scream could be heard from shore. R. P. is on top of a large school. Fishing off the bow. He's casting a popper and truly killing it. He gives an uncaring glance back at Snappy and keeps on doing his thing.

Once again, I know what he's thinking. *He's your fucking friend.* So I give Snappy the bait knife and tell him to work on it for a while.

"It's in there good," he said.

I grabbed the needle-nose pliers. Snappy has fear in his eyes.

"Don't pull it," he said.

"I'm just going to wiggle it just a li'l bit," I replied.

Whammo! I pulled on that thing so fucking hard, the meat and skin stretched out a few inches like it was a cartoon.

"Owww!"

"Hook out!"

Got out the first aid kit. Put some iodine on it. Followed by one of the two Band-Aids in the first aid kit. Gave him a beer and back to fishing we went.

Now bear in mind, these are all true stories. The following year, same cast of characters. Snappy reels in a fish. I didn't even finish the sentence.

"Don't forget to put the fish down. Remember what happened?"

"Owww!"

Same look from R. P. *It's your fucking friend.*

There goes Band-Aid number two.

Gaspar holding a fifty pound + striped bass
caught off Martha's Vineyard

Marine 13

For the record, I support all veterans and the armed forces.

So this 24-7 marginally intoxicated *regular* hears about my aspirations to write a memoir about my day-to-day observations. So my customer—I'll call him Marine 13—wants, insists, and wishes to be in "my pages."

Well, let's see. Marine 13 is a lanky six feet two and maybe 150 pounds. The pencil in my hand has more meat and grit. Most marines are hard as nails. Marine 13 is as soft as a pillow. Besides his admiration for the booze, which is good for my cash register, he's been slowly succumbing to the worst disease ever—lazy-itus.

So I'm thinking of helping my customer on two fronts.

I'm putting him in my book. Plus, I am putting him to work.

I am going to give "*you*," the reader, permission to rip out this page. Fold it several times and use it as a bookmarker.

Speech

None warranted. Start folding!

Footnote:

I find it imperative to add an addendum to *"Marine 13."*

That short story was written over eight years ago at the height of my boozing-asshole ways.

Marine 13 has been dead for several years now. Another cautionary tale of alcohol abuse.

I thought of throwing it out. Respectfully, for his family. But he was there at the inception of my first writings and was adamant that

I write about him. Even if it was like I said, "Going to be honest and a little unflattering."

"I don't care about all that, as long as I am in it."

RIP, A. C.

Jackknife in Your Sweaty Hands

It was the middle of the week. Same old bullshit. Then two unknown faces walked in and make a beeline to the bathroom. Really? You're going to pull your drug dealing shenanigans in my bar? They picked the wrong bar.

I went into the bathroom. I didn't knock. I walked in there like I own the place. Wait a minute. I do own the place.

I walked in there and smacked whatever their shit was straight into the toilet.

Flush…have a good day, losers. They mumble some FU's under their breath and walked out.

Now it becomes a pissing match. The further they get down the block, the braver they get. The fuck yous get louder. Cocky little bastards.

"Fuck yous!"

"No, fuck you."

And then it happened. Somebody said, "Your mother!"

Oh, fuck no. Not in my world.

They think that two blocks distance is going to be their saving grace. Not today. Not any day.

Every person with a semblance of street wisdom knows people get hurt for uttering those two words. I'm sure there are mothers out there that ain't worth a shit. But my mom was a churchgoing charitable warm soul. And she was full of the cancer. And I was full of the drink. And full of hate toward any disrespect.

Billy and Cool Tommy (C. T.) were recruited to come with me and go and talk to these fools about respect. No words were needed to be discussed in the short ride to intercept these idiots, who for all intents and purposes probably thought they were home free.

Wrong.

So here is what I remember about our talk with these assholes. We pulled right beside them a few blocks up the road. They were still smiling, taking delight in disrespecting a total stranger. Say hello to my little friend. His name is called street justice.

C. T. unleashed a one-two punch and tossed this unconscious dickhead into a telephone pole to drive home our message of respect. His job was done. And done fast. I was impressed with his social skills and how he helped this misguided youth find his path. Straight into the gutter.

Now I and Billy are helping bozo number two see the error of his ways.

Unbeknownst to us, he had a box cutter. That's a straight-up razor. Regardless, he would have had better luck with a gun and a grenade.

Well, Billy got a slice to the torso, and me? I should have done "paint the fence." Instead of a "wax on." Anyways, this punk got smacked up good and ran up the street and left his friend passed out in the gutter. I think our talk went pretty well.

I didn't even know I was sliced up until I saw the blood squirting on my hood and then there was that distinctive smell. It's akin to a metallic iron scent. And it's something I've spilled more times than I care to think about.

Fast forward. I'm at the hospital getting my forearm stapled. Cool. Some guys get tattoos, I collect scars.

The emergency room tech left me alone in the room and left a fifty-milliliter bottle of pharmaceutical lidocaine. How it fell in my pocket, I have no idea. But it came in handy two weeks later when I took the staples out myself with a pair of needle-nose pliers. Lidocaine is used as a local anesthetic. You don't get high on it. But it will numb you up well wherever you inject it.

The detectives came in to talked to me and wanted my assurance that there would be no further escalation or payback.

Nah! I'm good. I just wanted to talk to these young men about respect and having some manners. In retrospect, I think all parties involved came away with some lessons and certain truths.

A few people told me I should have let them just walk away and swallowed my pride. Yeah, maybe. And that would have been the end of it. But what these people don't understand is that an invisible line in the sand was crossed.

The minute they muttered, "your mother," it was game on. Win, lose, or draw. And I'll do it again if I need be. I'm Catholic. I do subscribe to turn the other cheek. But I'm also human. And I come with all the frailties that it entertains.

When they put me in the ground, I want them to say, "There's a man in that hole."

In conclusion, when the time came to take the staples out, my wife wanted me to go to the clinic. "And what? Pay two hundred bucks?" Fuck that!

Patrick. The snowblower guy was sitting next to me at the bar. I said, "Let's go, McGoogle! We'll grab a twelve-pack and take care of this ourselves."

My wife was still yelling as we drove away.

Well, I injected one cc in both sides of the scar and drank a few beers, and in no time at all, my forearm was so numb I could grate cheese off those staples.

Now in a hospital setting, there's a special tool that is used to remove staples. We used pliers. Different approach, same results. But when Patrick recounts the story, he tells people I cried like a little girl. This guy cracks me up. Maybe I'll staple his nutsack to his leg. Then we'll see who cries like a little girl.

Fucking Patrick. He's lucky he's my friend. Or maybe he's not so lucky. You'll have to ask him.

5/15/2021

FTD Lover Boy

Jimmy, Jimmy, Jimmy…what are we going to do with you? First off, I don't have anything derogatory to write about this man. Aside from his bad luck with women, I find him to be an affable fellow. Always smiling, and I enjoy our back-and-forth ribbing. I was even told that he's a preacher or reverend. I should know these things, but I exude apathy like sweat on a decathlon athlete's back. I really don't care about the whos or the whats about people. I personally go with "the less I know the better" philosophy, which either makes you appear trustworthy or just an uncaring, selfish prick. And I'm totally fine with both perceptions because as long as my wife and dog love me… I'm happy and all's well in Al Swain's world.

Now, Mr. Jimmy, besides being a friend of Jesus, also has lots of love for beer and the ladies. And one of his favorite crushes is my wife. He's got a good taste because my wife is a beautiful girl and an even more beautiful person.

I'm not jealous. It's actually complimentary. Besides, I don't find Jimmy either a threat or the "creepy guy." And if the missus was ever going to leave me, she could've and would've a long time ago. I don't call her my "long-suffering wife" for nothing. Unfortunately, the world isn't full of nonthreatening Jimmys. If and when I do hear a disparaging, sexist remark toward my wife, well…let's just say I relish my role as protector.

Now Jimmy's idiosyncrasy is to give any lady that shows him the slightest bit of kindness a bouquet of flowers. And not the cheap kind, but the kind that comes in a classy basket or vase and screams that it cost over fifty dollars. Fine, whatever gets you through the night, right? He's like a sixty-year-old cupid bearing flowers instead of a bow and arrow and a diaper. And I'm not 100 percent sure about the diaper.

Sorry, I had to pause to take a long sip of my drink.

Anyways, the girls love it. Even though I've never seen it get him any closer to a honey hole, I must still give him an "*A*" for effort.

Now, this one time, he brings into the bar a nice arrangement and says they're for my wife. I did not take umbrage at this but instead, decided to flip the script on him and amuse myself at the same time. I was feeling a little sportive. Perhaps because I had imbibed in a few Bacardi Cokes.

Nonetheless, right in front of Jimmy, I said, "Wow, cool, I haven't given my long-suffering wife flowers in a while. She's abso-fuck-ing-lutely going to love the fact that I got her this sign of endearment for no particular reason and on a Tuesday no less. Thanks, Jimmy."

He chuckled haphazardly but his smile was soon waning when, without skipping a beat, I tossed his card and replaced it with one of my own.

"You wouldn't dare," he quipped.

"I am, and I just did. I'm sorry...did I forget to say thank you? Thank you."

"She'll never believe you!" he said in dismay.

"Probably not, but it's worth a try, and that's what you get for giving another man's wife flowers," I said with a sly smirk. "She's going to love them." I only added that last sentence to turn the knife a little deeper in his back.

And she did love them. And on a Tuesday, no less. I was the cat's meow. Thank you, Jimmy.

But my wife wasn't without her doubts, so I gave her an Oscar-winning performance.

"Does a husband need a holiday or any reason, for that matter, to get the one he adores flowers any day of the week? Coming to work this morning, I saw a beautiful sunrise and it reminded me of you, that's all." Ahhh, perfect and less is more. Let's keep the lies short and sweet for future recall.

She was my queen, and I was her knight in shining armor.

Until...and it was about a week later. I got the phone call.

"Who really brought me those flowers?" she asked.

"Me…why?" feeling my armor cracking.

"Is Jimmy there? Because he's a jealous guy and said he was going to try and take credit for the flowers. He bought the flowers, didn't he?" asked my long-suffering wife.

"Um…yeah." Reconciled to the fact that the "jig is up."

"Sunset, flowers on a Tuesday, I knew I smelled a rat," she said, pained.

Thank you, Jimmy, FTD Lover Boy, and your big mouth. The gall of this guy. Taking credit for his own flowers.

And His Mama Cries

Anthony and I came up with a saying to separate the good women from the bad. We've been tossing this saying around for thirty years. I would start the first sentence and he would finish the last. It went something like this:

"Are you my mother?"

(No.)

"Go stand in the comer with the rest of the ——!"

We would use a more stinging word after "the."

Anthony and I were mama's boys for real. And our mamas loved us to the tenth degree. Squared and multiplied by a million.

His poor mom would actually wait outside bars for him, and I am not kidding. She would wait for hours. Plus, she would call him a hundred times. He would tell me to say that he wasn't here. And I'm like "Really, dude? She's outside the door looking right at us."

Anthony's mom has been dead for many years now. And he'll look outside the door's window and there is no one looking back. Real love. A mother's love. Unwavering.

Now Anthony gets married some years back. Love is blind. Why is that? Outsiders knew it wasn't going to work. I made book on the over/under on the number of years before it would all implode and turn to shit.

We all told him. Right up to the church. Right in the limo. "You sure about this, bud? It's not too late to bail. We can take this limo up to the casino."

I think maybe, deep down, he did second-guess himself. But he went through with it, nonetheless.

Just like me and my first wife. That's another story. We have children together, so I will not begrudge her but say "Thank you for my great kids." And that's all I got to say about that.

So I'll part on another saying we bounce around a lot:

Next time, "Get a tattoo. It lasts longer."

Today is Good Friday, April 2, 2021.

For Mom:

I often stop and think about you.

Puffing on the Mary Jane

Once a raisin…you can't go back to being a grape.

But you got to believe. You got to have faith. If a man, two thousand years ago, could turn water into wine, then you too can rise up from the ashes. Like a caterpillar. Free yourself.

"Flying High Again"

again

again

Words Are All I've Got

Words. They're just fucking words strung together to form sentences. They inform, express, give direction, reflect, make us laugh and cry. C. T. once told me to write about him. He's a good kid, well-liked by most. "Live voraciously through me," I believe he said. Now why the fuck would I do that when I got a lifetime of words and stories?

But my mind spins. When will all my words be strung together in one of the many trillions of combinations? When there are no more lyrics to write one more song?

"To be or not to be." Simple pretentious bullshit. But it is revered because it comes from the hand of a true storyteller. So I ponder, *When is every possible sentence or lyric going to be written down?*

When free speech is no longer free. Every single word will be copy-written and owned. Bought, sold, and traded. Open your eyes, America. Pretty soon, you won't be able to say "Good morning" without paying someone for the privilege because you fucking strung two words together that someone owns.

Bye-bye, First Amendment. Once the first domino falls, the rest will follow.

8/9/21

In for a Penny

In for a penny, in for a pound
Streets always watching, looking all around
One drink too many, a thousand not enough
Those who peacock, run when it gets tough
Smiles in the front, whispers behind your back
Some will always try, while others only lament
So why all the pain and so little merit?
The proud will be humbled and the meek shall inherit

February 27, 2016

Hoopah Drives the Boat

So it's no secret. I fucking love *Jaws* and *Rocky I* and *II*. I've watched each one hundreds of times. Every time, whenever, always period.

So customers would moan, "Not this movie again."

"Muthafuckers…if you don't like it, buy your own fucking bar." This ain't Applebees.

I don't subscribe to the customer-is-always-right rule. If that was true, these fucks would want to drink for free.

I had my DNA done. Apparently, I have royal blood as well as…the third-highest Neanderthal blood out of one thousand, five hundred cousins I've never met. Fucking cool. Now that's what we would call a paradox. It would explain why my brother is so hairy. I'm talking…hairy-like-a-gorilla hairy. We would have to hose him down during the dry season. One spark and he'd go up like a tinder box. Where am I going with this?

So every night, I'd watch *Jeopardy*. And I would kill it. Impressing everyone who's probably not even paying attention. But one person was—Nick at Nite. This fucking guy was smart.

While I'm picking potpourri for $200, he's picking seventeenth-century authors for $1000.

"Who is Jonathon Swift?"

"Muthafucka. You didn't? Fuck that, I think there's a *Rocky* movie on."

It's my bar. This guy's not going to steal my thunder. Poor Nick. Everybody liked this guy. And he loved my wife and me. He was truly a good person. I have yet to find a regular customer who operated at his intellectual level. Many nights, I'd let him sleep in one of my empty rentals. We wouldn't let him drive home drunk. He was family.

So here's another interesting tidbit. In Florida, *Jeopardy* came on first. Then *Wheel of Fortune*.

Up north in Massachusetts, it was the complete opposite. *Wheel* first, *Jeopardy* second. I would text somebody for the answers to the final *Wheel of Fortune* puzzle and the final *Jeopardy* answer. And for what? To impress my parents? They're asleep in their chairs. I would cheat. Even though I didn't have to. Insecure, neanderthal narcissistic? Yep, that's me.

Back to the movie, *Jaws*. Me and my best bud, R. P., would take my boat out. He would chirp nonstop, "Hoopah, hoopah." We cracked ourselves up as good friends do over tiniest and dumbest of shit.

Yo, Adrian…we're gonna need a bigger boat.

RIP

Nicholas B.

4/27/21

BFF

Mr. Ron Bacardi and Classic Coke. Yeah. It was Ron Bacardi forever as long as I could remember. Now it's just Bacardi. I don't know why they dropped the Ron name part. Maybe they had a falling out or something.

I got an old bottle. I'll take a picture because young people don't remember that.

Anyways, three fingers of Bacardi in a highball glass, lots of ice, top it off with Classic Coke, no lime, no straw. Done.

I once had a bad experience with a straw. I was talking to a girl in some bar, many moons ago. And I go down for a sip and the straw goes right up my nose. She walked away and I've had some hate issues with straws ever since.

But I've always had a love affair with my Bacardi Cokes. Maybe they can pick up the tab on my new liver. Good times, bad times. My friend has always been near and dear to me. Just don't drive or beat up your wife with your friend and you'll be fine.

As a footnote, one of my few, true, flesh-and-blood friends since kindergarten is also named Ron. Such a good friend he was, best man at my wedding. I, real Ron, and Bacardi flew to Tampa for my bachelor party. I was told I had a great time.

Speech

If you could be so kind and bear with me a minute. I'd like to introduce a dear, good friend of mine.

Mr. Ron…(pause) Bacardi.

(Hilarious when done in the presence of real Ron)

She Ain't No "Maid of Honor"

"With your long blonde hair. And your eyes of blue. The only thing I ever got from you was sorrow" (David Bowie).

Tony would play this song every time at the bar. Dedicated to his ex-wife. I collected on my book from all the suckers who took the over.

She got passed around freely of her own accord. It'll probably be faster to say who didn't make her acquaintanceship. She was pretty. And she gave it away far too easy. Cocaine is a hell of a drug. Last I heard, she got help and was doing better. Good for her. Everyone's deserving of redemption and a second chance. Including Yours Truly.

She was a friends "Maid of Honor."

And that always throws me back to the Sopranos episode where Christopher Moltisanti tells his fiancée, "She ain't no Maid of Honor." Fuckin loved that show. Shitty ending.

RIP "James Gandolfini."

So this brings me back to Snappy Pappy.

Where did he get that nickname? I gave it to him. The Snappy part was simple. He wasn't the sharpest tool in the woodshed. It was a play on words. Like fat guys named "Tiny."

And the Pappy? This is sad. He starts living with Tony's ex-wife and her children fathered by two different men.

So this femme fatale, I dubbed her "Banana Split." I'm not even going to get into how she earned that nickname.

So this girl makes Snappy babysit her brood every Friday night and makes a beeline to my house. The guys and I used to play poker every Friday and drink and do other things.

Around midnight, my phone rings. It's Snappy.

"Hey, sorry to bother you is ———— there? The kids are crying, and I can't put them to sleep.

Without hesitation, I say, "Yeah, she's here. She's free to leave whenever she wants, but this bitch wants to stay all night."

"Can you tell her that the kids want her home?"

"Sure thing, Pappy. But I wouldn't wait up if I was you."

Upon Us All a Little Rain Must Fall

I forgive those that let me astray. And I beg for forgiveness from all those that I led astray.

Anger and hate are akin to letting someone live rent free in your head.

It all starts with an olive branch. But don't get me wrong. There are people out there that I would love to beat to an inch of their lives. I'm only human. I'm trying my best. Live and let live.

"And to you who are troubled, rest with us when the Lord Jesus shall be revealed from Heaven with his mighty Angels" (2 Thessalonians 1:7).

3/12/21

I Got a Speech for That

"I'd like to thank the Big Guy, my mom and dad, my long-suffering wife, the members of the academy."

The crowd goes wild. Why the speech? Did I win some coveted award? Oscar, Emmy? Nope, none of the above. Something even better.

I won Final *Jeopardy*.

What was the name of Alexander the Great's father?

Who is Philip II of Macedon?

Easy breezy. Well, it should be. I suffered through the movie with Colin Farrell and Val Kilmer as Philip II. There goes more than two hours of my life I'll never get back.

But did I win an actual something, anything? Yes, indeed. I won the accolades of my peers. Albeit, my peers this evening are a husband and wife nursing a couple of brews at the end of the bar. So what? They're entertained and laughing. Or are they laughing at me? Do I really care?

Yes, I do care. And the moment is ripe to do my "faux speech." And using my utmost, theatrically gifted skill set, I pretend to reach into my back pocket and pull out an imaginary stack of speeches. Yes, stack. Then I'll lower my eyeglasses down the bridge of my nose just so. And pretend to peruse through a nonexistent stack of speeches for all occasions.

Damn, here's my Spelling Bee victory speech.

Ahhh…memories. "I wish to thank my adversary, Kapur, for taking his loss in the utmost, honorable fashion…"

Poor Kapur. Sucks that your word was PARASTRATIOSPHECOMYIA STRATIOSPHECOMYIOIDES. A species of soldier fly, native to Thailand. Shit, everybody knows that.

In Kapur's defense, his shortcoming was that he forgot that very last "*I*." Gets them every time. P.S. My word was "fruit fly."

Why the name Kapur? Simple, I'm stereotyping. There's always a kid from India standing up there in the top three. They must love their spelling bees.

Enough with the "faux speeches." My wife and I run a small bar. Even though I've lost some passion for my work, I haven't lost my love for imbibing with my good friend, Bacardi Coke.

Booze is some sort of a cosmic bonus. I say bonus because some days are great and uneventful. And others are filled with fools, gobble-gook nonsense. You can't argue with a fool. It's futile. But a few stiff drinks and…if you can't beat them, join them.

But the "good ole days" are just that. Past tense. Fucking bills and taxes just to pay the masses.

My wife and I work every day just to keep payroll and shrinkage to a minimum and to keep our eyes on the prize. That whole "while the cat's away" bullshit. Those mice, they do like to fucking play.

It's hard to find honest, hardworking people nowadays. But we do have a few good eggs who help us out. And to them…thank you. Yous know who you are.

About twenty years ago, I was regaling one of my true drunken yarns to my friend. He said I was funny. I jokingly told him that I was going to write a book. He said, "Go for it, kid. Seriously, go for it."

Okay, I'm going for it. For starters, no real names to protect the guilty. And I'm pretty sure most of these fucks are guilty of something. And as far as the innocent go…what do they care?

Some people actually implore me to use their real names. I guess they wish to live through my pages of unpolitically *correct* tales.

Fine by me. Buckle up. What a boring existence it would be to live a life without a few memorable stories.

Melancholy Rock

It's a gloomy, rainy Thursday morning. I feel a wave of depression washing over me. My spirit is being swallowed up. Like a rock being smothered by the rising tide.

Sometimes, I wish I could just disappear. But I can't because I'm afraid.

And I can't believe I'm the one writing this. But I see my hand, and the words are coming from my brain. But who am I? A stranger to myself.

For now, I must wait. Wait for the tide to go out and for the sun to shine on my rock. Melancholy is fleeting. I must hold fast and bide my time till it passes.

Maybe I don't have depression. Maybe I'm just plain sick and tired of being sick and tired. Maybe I just want to concede and throw in the towel.

Tired of paying bills. Tired of going to work every day. Tired of saying "Thank you" and "You're welcome" a hundred times, day in and day out. It's my ticket and I want to get off this ride.

I think I'll go hide until the tide goes out.

Speech

Pick yourself up by the bootstraps and man up. Sick and tired? I'm sick and tired of all your bellyaching.

Dog Day Sunny Afternoon

January 5, 2016. Happy fucking new year. Got to make some changes. Maybe I'll quit drinking. My long-suffering wife is getting tired of my antics.

Quit drinking? Who am I fucking kidding? My crappy writing would become official crappy writing. What the hell am I supposed to pen to paper so I can fill a book of vaguely amusing stuff that somebody would actually pay money for?

I mean, I'd read it. Some of this shit is funny and it's my life. That has to account for something, right?

But what would I say to people who've said they have read my book and "by the way, I found it in a box marked FREE SHIT at some yard sale"? But that would mean somebody, somewhere actually paid good money for my musings.

Cool! What's not so cool is that someone came across it unceremoniously discarded inside a FREE SHIT box at some yard sale. My book would probably be under some old Rubik's Cube with half the stickers peeled off. Like some metaphor for my life.

Well, tonight, I'm writing from my couch. And my rescue dog, Sunny, is eyeballing me from her couch. Go ahead, ask her. Actually, it's her house. And my long-suffering wife and I are lucky that she's kind enough to let us live here with her.

I'm sober tonight. Maybe that's good. Maybe it's bad. Not sure. Not sure I care. I think the dog prefers happy me because it translates into more snacks and praise. But it's a little one-sided. I've never seen her pick up the tab.

I solved tonight's final *Wheel of Fortune* puzzle. Yay! Almost by reflex, or my OCD, I was going to recite one of my obligatory, congratulatory speeches. But what's the use. I'm home alone watching television in my underwear, and I'm pretty sure my dog could care less that I solved a game show puzzle.

Yep, she just licked herself, jumped off the couch, and went to chew on her squeaky. Maybe she is impressed? I'll try my speech on her anyways! What's the worst she can say? "You suck."

"Oh yeah!" I'll angrily retort with a loathing tone.

"No snacks for you." That'll teach her.

After all, I do appreciate her input. Really, who's the smart one in this relationship? I'm the fool who goes to work all day, every day. All she does is sleep on her couch, live in a nice house, two square meals a day. Of course, the gourmet dog food. Air conditioning, HBO, and Netflix. Plenty of "good girl" praise.

Fuck me! Maybe we can trade for a day. She can go and do my job, and I'll stay home and practice making sad faces in the mirror. Which I surmise she does because she's damn good at it when she wants to steal away a table scrap.

Remember, a spouse may throw you to the curb, but a good dog will lie in the gutter with you.

Don't forget to spay and neuter.

Sunshinze, AKA Sunny Dummy

The King(s) of Cool

I decide what is right and
what is wrong and I don't
have to explain it to
anybody.

I like women, but I'm a little
afraid of them. I'm not
going to make a commitment
because if you make a
commitment to a woman
they can hurt you.

I won't pick a fight. But if
you pick a fight with me
or back me into a corner,
I will fucking kill you!

(Steve McQueen's Mantra)

Little Darling

Let's roll it back to 1984, what I would call the good old days.

I was a tall lanky kid with the Vinnie Barbarino hair. Maybe fourteen to fifteen years old.

So I hear about a kegger just down at the end of the block at the former NB Yacht Club.

I'm a freshman in high school and in one of my study halls was the sweetest thing. She was a junior. That two-year age difference. Might as well be a chasm as big as the Grand Canyon.

An older woman… I'm not talking about "Mrs. Robinson old." But as a young man, anyone two years older than you was your peer.

So this beautiful girl says hi to me one day. We begin talking and I mentioned this party. I didn't have a car, so I couldn't pick her up. If she shows. She shows.

But I did what I do best. It was the butterfly effect.

On the day of the party, I rode my bike to "Ocean Meadows." Sounds nice, huh? Maybe an over fifty-five community in Vero Beach Florida.

Wrong. It was the projects. Our own little Afghanistan. One unfortunate guy got beat to death just because he had a flat tire on "their turf."

So I ride my bike in there and buy a hit of mescaline. What happened to mescaline? It was everywhere. Then it was gone. Just like quaaludes.

So the night of the party, I showered. Splashed on the Brut Cologne and tossed that mescaline tab down my throat.

"Bye, Mom."

"Bye, *meu querido filho*. Be careful. I'll pray for you."

Good, Jesus can come with me too. I just don't have any mescaline for him.

I walk the five minutes down to the yacht club. The door charge was only five bucks. But I did not have to pay because I got there right when the guest of honor arrived—a full barrel of Budweiser.

Guy yells at me, "Hey kid, help me carry this barrel down the stairs."

"Yeah sure."

That guy a few years later married my cousin. Small world.

Well now, I'm at the party and even helped out the cause. So I didn't see any reason to pay the five bucks nor did anybody notice or care.

I quickly chugged a few beers and passed around what seemed like endless joints. The band started playing. I was exuding testosterone-one-filled confidence with the wisp of vulnerability.

But confidence was fleeting. Like a light switch, something happened. And I knew exactly what it was. I felt an encompassing dread. So much fun. And then that fucking mescaline crippled me. I and the wall were both cosmically holding each other up. I couldn't move. I couldn't make a complete sentence. I was more than happy to just be.

Now here comes the embarrassing part. The girl…from study hall. She sees me and is definitely glad to bump into a familiar face.

She says, "Hi, Al, want to dance?"

I shook my head, and my eyes most definitely gave me away.

Boy, did I fuck up. If I played my cards right and never took that mescaline, I would've taken this beautiful creature for a stroll on the beach. Who knows? Funny how you do one thing at a junction of your life, and it has real consequences, good and bad.

My walk home was lonely and seemed to take forever. But I did make it home. I avoided my mother. She was asleep, thank God.

She would've taken one look at my eyes, and the jig would be up. I stayed up all night with my thoughts racing, thinking about what could have been.

And that pretty girl. Never talked to me again.

3/5/21

She Thinks I'm Cute

"She thinks I'm cute!"

"She thinks I'm cute!"

Sac used to do that spot on. The line from *Rudolph the Red-Nosed Reindeer*. Another one he did was:

"We represent the Lollipop Guild, the Lollipop Guild, the Lollipop Guild."

You'd think the *Wizard of Oz* was on TV.

The girls loved it. Hell, guys loved it. And when Sac was feeling good, we all had a great fucking time.

Being a purveyor of alcoholic beverages for over thirty years, you become a great observer of people and what makes them tick.

It took about eight Bud Lights to bring "fun Sac" out.

Sac was a soul with many thoughts and few words. Being a Vietnam Vet impacted him on a deep, personal plane. I never wished to examine his reflections and he was more than fine with that.

He went to fight wars for lying kings. Came back stateside soaked in Agent Orange, painful memories, and to a country that showed him no honor and no glory.

But he always had a friend at the bar.

Sac would come into the bar same time every day. It was hard to miss his truck with the American flag he proudly flew on his antenna.

He wouldn't say much right away. Sometimes, not even a hello. But eight beers later and my friend was back.

"Love you, man," he would say. And he meant it. Some guys need to lubricate and decompress. I get it. Shit, I do the same.

Booze…isn't it great?

Speech

To all my real friends…here's to those who wish us luck.
The rest can go and get fucked.
Hip, hip, hoorah! Drink up!
Muthafuckas.
"*Mike Sacs birthday party*" on YouTube.
At 3:53 VIDEO.
Notable VIPs:

- Sacco
- Long Suffering Wife
- Pollack
- Smiling Bob and Pamela
- Snappy Pappy
- Nick at Nite
- Jimmy FTD

Music Icons

Elvis and the Beatles. In that order. Well, the Beatles…what's there to say? Musical geniuses. I personally believe Ringo (real name, Richard Starky) will be the last living Beatle standing. I was lucky to see Paul McCartney in Boston years back. I was less than fifty feet away from a living Beatle. Definitely will be imprinted in my brain's hard drive forever.

Elvis, a poor boy plucked out of obscurity and abject poverty. While just barely into manhood, he's handed the keys to the kingdom. I'm surprised he lived as long as he did. Even toward the end, his God-given voice never wavered. Heavy is the head that wears the crown.

When I'm feeling nostalgic, the jukebox songs that came out from my pop's bar in the seventies. I'm talking about Harry Chapin and Jim Croce. Those songs bring me back to a more carefree time.

And when I just want to rock out… Led Zeppelin, baby! Full volume. Blast that shit. Many speakers have died to "Houses of the Holy."

"Where is that confounded bridge?"

3/8/21

Going to Massachusetts

"Thank you for flying Southwest…" You're welcome.

I've flown a couple of dozen times. Most flights were uneventful, which is the way I like it. But this last flight, Orlando to Providence, was just the opposite.

It was a night flight, and oh boy, do I love those night flights.

Cabin dimly lit, plenty of seating… I got my window seat. The middle seat was unoccupied, and the wife got the aisle seat. Dream configuration. Perfect night? Almost, and it wasn't the airline's fault, but the passenger in the row directly in front of us that we held disdain for.

I'll call him Mr. Gassy for all intents and purposes. Now, after the first fart, the wife and I were wondering, *What the fuck is that smell?* We didn't say it loudly, but we didn't say it under our breaths either. If I and the missus have something to say, we say it. Plus, I had a tall Bacardi Coke at the airport pub…make it a double for an extra buck. Well, why not? It's already seven dollars for a single.

Back to Mr. Gassy. We were going to give him the benefit of the doubt. Let's be honest, everybody lets one loose accidentally or even intentionally now and then. But the flatulence was an exceptionally horrible death fart that drifted back a few rows, and we didn't want people thinking it came from our row.

And it crept back like a dark cloud, and you could hear people behind whispering, "What the fuck is that smell?" The wife and I pointed in unison at Mr. Gassy, like fingering a perp in a lineup. Fuck him.

PFFFTH. No! Fuck me! Another one. The last fart is still lingering like swamp gas and now it's got reinforcements.

"Holy shit," pardon the pun, I say loudly. "Isn't this oxygen mask supposed to drop or something?" I'm banging on my overhead compartment like a mile-high Fonzie looking for some "cool" fresh air.

I looked over at my wife and she is gagging, all thanks to this inconsiderate asshole. Passengers four rows back are complaining. Heads are searching for a culprit. And that's when it happens.

PFFFTH. Not again! Fuck me!

That's it! I tattletaled. I hit the stewardess button and she came right over.

"Hi folks, can I help you? God, what the heck is that smell?" the stewardess asked, almost stunned like someone pepper-sprayed her. This poor woman probably thought that someone smuggled a skunk, shit, and two-week-old lobster shells in a carry-on bag.

Nope. Mystery solved. Me, the wife, and the last three rows pointed like a compass at true North aka Mr. Gassy.

"Can somebody hang some of them pine air freshener thingies around here please, and thank you?" And I wasn't kidding.

Where I come from, snitching is frowned upon. But something about taking away a person's freedom to breathe in clean, fresh air and we were all first graders tattling on Mr. Gassy. This crowd was judge and jury and ready to quarter this asshole. Maybe because he didn't even acknowledge all the harm he had done to all of our olfactory senses.

No. He just sat there. Didn't say a word. No "I'm sorry," no "I got this rare farting disease." Nothing. He just stared straight ahead and farted. Almost like he was having fun. Now we're, us, the last three rows, are going to have fun with "Mr. Gassy Crappy Dukey Pants."

The stewardess ran away. I assumed to throw up. But she came back. Damn, this bitch must be a Navy Seal. This angel of a stewardess returned. And she returned with a can of air freshener and liberally dispensed its contents up and down the aisle of said-affected rows all around Mr. Gassy. And as a sign of solidarity, she sprayed over his head from behind while winking at us because she felt our pain and was just as appalled and disgusted.

Ahhh…thank you, Glade Fresh Linen Scent.

And thank you, Ms. Southwest stewardess for the complimentary drinks. It wasn't necessary, but it shows that you care about your job and your customers. And it once again reaffirmed to me that it's not all pie in the sky when you work with the public.

Ding…thank you for flying Southwest!

No, thank you. We've landed. Our section clapped. The front of the plane was totally oblivious to the drama and small crises that unfolded in rows B-28 through B-31.

Speech

I want to thank…ahh, screw it. I just want to get off this plane so I can breathe again.

Gone Girl

Who writes these movies? Fucked up shit.

Amazing Amy… What a *C!*

Tyler Perry…you play a more convincing lawyer than an old, Black lady in drag. You got range, my man. No doubt.

Neil Patrick Harris…perfect guy to play the creep. "Octopus and Scrabble." What a douche. I heard that he added magician to his résumé. Good…maybe he can make Doogie Howser disappear.

Ben Affleck…local boy done good. Good for you, brother. If Matt Damon goes missing, call me. I'll roll with you. Always double down on eleven.

And last but not least, fake and real Nancy Grace. I feel for your husband. Poor bastard. Let's hope one of the twins doesn't grow up to be a serial killer. Now that would be a ratings bonanza.

Speech

I apologize. I'm not a real movie critic. I just play one on TV.

Va Com Deus

"*Va com Deus*," translated means "Go with God."

When they execute people in modern times, they are usually asked if they would like to give a last statement. It's usually a self-serving sorry many years too late. But I'm not their judge. Lest I be judged.

> A crucified dying thief turned to a man on the cross and said, "Jesus, remember me when you come into your kingdom."
>
> He answered him, "In truth I tell you, today you will be with me in paradise." (Luke 23:42–43)

Va com Deus.

Just Throwing Out the Garbage

I became complicit in my ways. On a beautiful Sunday morning, I stepped out my kitchen door to discard a wastebasket in the dumpster. And at that very moment, I caught the parking ticket guy starting to write me up for parking two wheels on my sidewalk.

"Don't you even dare," I muttered, just authoritative enough without sounding threatening. Nobody wants to go to jail on a Sunday morning.

But he was scared. He reached for his radio. Almost by instinct and sheer loathing, I said, "Who you gonna call, your mommy?"

I wasn't drinking. I wasn't in a bad mood. It's just the world once again putting its square peg in my one-way brain. Destiny or innate?

I park on the sidewalk because it's a narrow street and my favorite Chevy step side has been hit on that corner a couple of times already. Once by a Budweiser delivery truck. Got a new paint job out of that one. There's plenty of illegally parked cars on North Front Street, but this simpleton doesn't have the balls to be ticketing cars on a guarded leery street. He wouldn't make it to his second car before real trouble would bear down on him. So he plays it safe and tickets hardworking business owners.

Luckily for the meter boy of more than fifty years of age, and I call him meter boy because meter man would be too good of a title for this man-child, Patrick tapped me on the shoulder and told me to go back inside. Maybe have a drink.

Good idea, I think to myself.

I tell Patrick under my breath that this guy is two seconds away from getting tossed in the dumpster.

You see, Patrick is a retired city employee and knows most of these people. He talked to the guy, and I got no ticket. He told the guy I'm sorry. Fuck that! I was not remorseful in the least.

Later, Patrick told me the guy is a poor bastard and he's been shot once already too. I left my empathy home that day and said maybe they should have shot him twice. But I did find some compassion for this guy. He was just doing his job. And when did this compassion encompass me? After my third rum and Coke.

This story could have had a couple of different outcomes. In canny hindsight, we came to an agreeable amicable conclusion. Momma says, "It's always best not to go to jail on the Lord's Day." That Momma. She's a wise one.

"Sac"

"Sac is missing," that's the call I got. Can't remember who called but it doesn't matter. I know that missing was the hopeful wording for what I knew it truly meant.

You see, Sac's been missing before. I suspect it was a trial run. The obligatory cry for help. But instead of falling on caring ears, we (I) mocked him. That's why I feel shame because I know about pain. I can't speak for his or anybody else's demons. But I know I've wanted to go missing myself. Run and hide with my depression and my pain.

But I'm scared and wish not to go missing, but to be found. Sanity likes to play hide and seek with my mind. Today, tomorrow, whatever, whenever. Doesn't really matter. The point is that for today, depression can't find me, and I'm still found and not missing.

Sac was a proud man. I knew he was hurting. I knew he was in financial trouble when he asked me to sign as a witness on a lien on his beloved Harley. A motorcycle that he had a lien, or sold, to my knowledge at least three times.

And I know when I signed that paper and he looked at me, that he was already missing.

My friend was found.

Alone and cold. Nobody knows what someone is thinking or the mental illness they're suffering.

I wish my friend was here now so I could say "I love you, Brother."

There is no fucking speech. We all dropped the ball and will carry our fair share of pain. Real friends look out for real friends.

Michael E. Mamaras (1952–2014).

Bar Fight

Lots of battles in the land of drink because cowards and punks love to mill around in the booze world. They feel safe to ply their ignorance. The blanket of imbibing gives these people courage.

STRIKE FIRST.

STRIKE FAST.

WTF

If you like to reflect on perplexing examinations like me, I suggest you refrain from doing the marching powder before you lay your head on your pillow. Stupid stuff. But I can't control my yearning for answers to some baffling WTF questions. So perplex me.

I'll write down a few. I'm sure thousands more have taken up rental space inside my gray matter.

1. I was watching an archaeological program where they were digging down. Always digging down. Forty feet is a few thousand years in our history. My question is, Where the Fuck does all this dirt come from? Did somebody forget to dust? If our planet is supposedly hundreds of millions of years old, that's a lot of dirt.

2. Electric cars. Great for the environment. Where the Fuck does the electricity come from? Let me guess. The coal-fired plant down the street? Never mind the pollution involved in making those batteries.

3. Where the Fuck does the universe end? And What the Fuck is one foot over the line?

4. Where the Fuck is the government hiding all the UFOs? Back engineering through private companies to circumnavigate the constitution. Beware the Industrial Military Complex. I bet half those things flying around are ours. Then waiting to implement a false flag and start their New World Order.

5. They have to be interdimensional or us coming back from the future. Either that or they're what? Drunk flying. You transverse a hundred million light-years of time and space

and then what? What the Fuck, did they forget to use their "blinkah"?

6. (I'm from the Boston area) and crash into a desert in New Mexico?

7. Let's not forget. Where's the Fucking complex tunnel system the government has crisscrossing this country? Earthquakes in the Ozarks every day. Yeah, okay.

8. I better stop while I'm ahead before who the fuck Men in Black show up in my rearview? They stole Tesla's notes. Goodbye, free energy. Not until big oil squeezes its last drop will they part with all the amazing new (old) discoveries and universal technologies.

9. The real Paul McCartney died in a car crash in 1967. Who the Fuck did I see in Boston? A McCartney look-alike contest winner named William Campbell? Some scalper owes me a refund.

10. Defund the police? Who the Fuck are you gonna call? Ghostbusters?

11. Fluoride is one of the most toxic, deadly chemicals known to man. Why the Fuck do they deem it necessary to put it in our drinking water?

12. What the Fuck is going on in Antarctica and why was Operation High Jump a failure? Because Admiral Richard E. Byrd supposedly got chased out by flying saucers?

13. Out-of-body experiences. I've had two. Once in a car wreck and the other one can be artificially induced. What the Fuck? I'm not going to mention how it's done. I saw my body. I saw and heard the people in the room. I will only say that it's called a "Rising Shotgun." I will not recommend anyone trying it. Serious, don't fuck around.

14. What the Fuck is going on with Denver International Airport, Skinwalker Ranch and Dulce, New Mexico?

15. What the Fuck happened to innocent until proven guilty?

16. Lastly, Why the Fuck does it always rain when I wash my car?

What the Cluck

Sunday morning, December 27. My friend, the "Polock," and I call him friend because he would probably cry and run away. And I do need the business. Serious, he is a friend.

Well, the Polock informs us through actual tears that "What the Cluck" has died.

"Who the fuck is 'What the Cluck'?" I curiously asked and definitely had to know.

Well, it seems that "What the Cluck" was one of his prized chickens. And until the coroner's report comes in, we surmise that "What the Cluck" either fell in with a bad crowd or didn't have a proper diet of greens and...umm...chicken.

Or was it something deeper? A darker secret that stole the spirit of dearly departed "What the Cluck." I'm talking about a heartache so deep, so painful, that only those that carry the pain, like an invisible cloak, know exactly what I'm talking about. A life unfulfilled. A "to-do list" that's never been fully checked off. Even if it's in one's own mind, it still bears the weight of the world.

Maybe poor "What the Cluck's" to-do list was simply "What's on the other side of that fucking road?" period. They do have small brains, for your information.

Enough with the dispatched chicken. I'm more worried about his human counterpart, the Polock. Will he take it like the 99 percent of the population who could care fucking less. Will he sink into a deep depression? A depression known only to those who've lost a special two-legged white meat friend. Only time will tell. In the meanwhile, I got a hankering for a bucket of Kentucky Fried Chicken.

While penning my "What the Cluck" chapter, I hardly noticed that Polack, my fowl-loving friend, had left crying. Maybe his sobbing will pay it forward, and in some strange way, his tears will unstick the stickiness of all the spilled drinks on my floor from the previous night. Cool, don't have to mop this morning.

I'd like to add that while he was here, he was a distraught empty vessel. Inconsolably reminiscing about sunny days gone by with his dead feathered friend.

But to the rest of us here, uncaring of his pain but still drinking strong. His chicken tale made for, at the very least, the funniest shit we heard this Sunday morning.

Take a Look at Yourself and You'll See Others Differently

Half a year until I finally punched through the other side. What did I do? It's personal. Let's just say it was a long time coming and I've found new reasons for living.

The second hardest thing I've ever had to do in my life. And I thank Jesus for freeing me from my chains. Now my job is to save others who ask for help. I'll throw them a life ring and a friendly ear. And the first thing I tell them is it's going to be the fight of your life. If it was easy, well, I think I've said it already, "Everybody would do it."

Now I can see clearly for the first time in forever.

4/16/2021

G-Man and the Loser Birds

G-Man is not a "Fed." He is a flesh-and-blood human being. I like this kid. He's me twenty years ago. He's a hard worker. Married and the next generation of good customers. But he's more than just a good customer. He's a good friend.

So this one Saturday morning, he comes in and he's looking a little pinkish around the gills.

I can smell the kerosene oozing from his pores.

"You okay, bud?" I ask. But I'm fully aware of what's ailing him. "Hanging around with those Loser Birds again?"

"Loser Birds? What's that?" Without batting an eye.

"You know when you're up all night doing that shit and right about 4:30–5:00 a.m., you hear the birds chirping?"

"Yeah," he quickly responds. "Those are loser birds?"

"No, brother. You are."

"You know what? You're right, my man."

"I know I'm right. I've heard them a million times. And I always felt like a loser when I hear these beautiful birds chirping away.

"The 'night' is almost finished, and the 'day' is almost here. So we should stop doing things that belong to darkness and take up the weapons used for fighting in the light" (Romans 13:12–14).

Take Me Home

Back to study hall. Damn…another study hall story. Why is a pointless high-school class that I skipped 99 percent of the time lived a .0001 percent of my life so memorable?

I'll tell you why. Crazy, memorable moments in time. One in particular was January 28, 1986, at 11:39 a.m.

So check this out. In my high school, there must be hundreds of rooms, classes, etc. The room adjacent is my English class. The teacher was Mr. M.

Now, Mr. M was one of the thousands of applicants for "Teacher in Space." Mr. M, my English teacher, made it to the top ten. NASA needed publicity for its fledgling space program, and our city and school needed just as much if not more during those days.

But NASA was a time capsule. All of the money was diverted to black ops. We were already in possession of antigravity, but I'll stop. Keep to the story.

So this vivacious, happy teacher gets picked and she was from a neighboring, adjacent state. Like Mr. M was in an adjacent room. Christa McAuliffe, wife, mother, daughter, and yes, teacher.

I remember the launch was postponed several times due to record cold temperatures in Florida. So one morning, they put these seven souls in a used car. What did they say in that movie? "A million moving parts put together by the lowest bidder."

The study room teacher, one morning, wheels in an old box television from the media room. Another great class to skip. That lady must have seen me five times all year and still passes me. Thank you, young red-headed lady. Sorry, forgot your name.

Now, because Mr. M was a big deal in this NASA program, they tried to get televisions in as many rooms as possible. This is before the internet, people. So a dozen of TVs went all over the school, which wasn't far. I usually sit in the back and sleep away my morning joint high. But today, I was going to sit in the front row.

Usually, there's a freshman in the front, so I told him to beat it. Big or small, it doesn't matter. They had to defer to rank and authority. I was a junior, and I had earned my time in the school hierarchy.

So anyway, I'm in the front row, TV right in front of me. Some prayer. Words of time of wonder and exploration are coming from the PA loudspeaker. But my eyes are fixed on that TV. Blast off! All righty, this has been cool. I'll wait five minutes and get a yellow bathroom pass and I'll be gone. Blast off morning joint fest number two.

Seventy-three seconds later, NASA engineer says, "Get ready to roll..." and *boom!*

Most viewers didn't really notice what was happening before their eyes. But I knew they were already dead.

RIP:

- *Christa McAuliffe*
- *Francis R. Scobee*
- *Michael J. Smith*
- *Ronald McNair*
- *Ellison Omizuka*
- *Judith Resnick*
- *Gregory Jarvis*

To Mr. M, I might have been the "stoner kid," but I did learn from you and a few others.

Thank you!

Let It Be

What's the old adage? Three can keep a secret if two are dead.

Well, I do know three. God. My dog. And the man in the mirror.

I walk softly now, and I don't need a big stick. And all of this...

Will be over when "he says it's over."

"For whoever calls upon the name of the Lord shall be saved" (Romans 10:13).

Get Back to Where You Once Belonged

My spirit was dead. But now it lives. I spent a small fortune on wine, women, and song. And the rest I squandered.

I'm just a stupid man. No more detours. Taking the long, hard, straight road. It has to be hard. If it was easy, everyone would do it.

Untie those ropes from the dock and cast off.

Now I'm underway. Don't know what's over the horizon. I'm scared, but as long as I stay in the light, I should not fear navigating any and all waters.

I have a new true north. My path has been revealed.

Stay the course. Sail to wherever you're welcomed and don't search for treasure on earth. One day, we all go away. Before I go. I leave you the worst of me. And the best of me. Also…

Getting here was hard. But honestly, I think staying here will be even harder. A bunch of chapters of a life. And in the end, does it even matter? I heard somewhere it's not how much you've loved, but how much you're loved. I like that. That's beautiful; somewhere between all these chapters is a human being. A son, husband, brother, father. I'm trying to atone, and I wish to entertain too. Take away what you like. Be good to each other. Peace.

The Work Doesn't Stop
till the Casket Drops

Who touched me
Who stood by me
Much love and thanks.
Mom, RIP
Dad, RIP
Vava, RIP
Sister
Wife
Daughter
Son
My beautiful granddaughter
Godfather and Godmother
I wouldn't dare use your real names because some may find my writings to be vulgar and dangerous.

Surely goodness and mercy shall follow me all the days of my life: And I will dwell in the house of the Lord forever. Psalm 23:6

Author's Note

I was asked to submit a glossy photo of myself when my book of short stories was green-lit for publication.

Half a year earlier, Shawn the Mailman asked me if I was still writing my book. I gave him my standard quintessential reply, "I stopped writing when my parents got sick."

I've been using that excuse for over seven years. But it was a half-truth. The other half that I shamefully kept to myself was that I had a big monkey on my back, and his good friend depression was tethered to him the entirety of their fellowship.

My mind was racing with thoughts, so I just started writing. I found my old writings. Hundreds of pages strewn between dozens of notebooks and a mishmash of cocktail napkins.

My wife types my stuff up. She looked at my thousands of pages of scribble and said, "No way!" So I gutted it. Wrote a few new short ones and with the spiritual intercession of a good friend, I found a new way to atone by leaving an uplifting passage at the end of some of my stories.

My friend wishes to stay anonymous. Anyone who is truly trying to do God's work doesn't look for earthly rewards and accolades. And neither do I.

If this book does well, I'll learn how to type and bring back some of the many stories I wish I could have put into this book. And maybe I'll add my photo. But in a world that loves to throw stones, I am happy to stay anonymously happy with my new life, my wife, and my dog.

God bless!

CPSIA information can be obtained
at www.ICGtesting.com
Printed in the USA
LVHW011053310322
714806LV00004B/792